So They Say You Should Write a Book

A new author's guide to writing a book
people will buy *and* read

JEVON BOLDEN
Best-selling editor and writer

SO THEY SAY YOU SHOULD WRITE A BOOK
Jevon Bolden

Published by Embolden Media Group
PO Box 953817
Lake Mary, FL 32795
emboldenmediagroup.com

Visit the author's website at jevonbolden.com.

While the author has made every effort to provide accurate internet addresses at the time of publication, neither the publisher nor the author assumes any responsibility for

International Standard Book Number: 978-1-7338730-5-5
Ebook ISBN: 978-1-7338730-4-8

19 20 21 22 23 — 987654321
Published in the United States of America

Contents

Introduction

Someone heard your story and said you should write a book. Is this true? Is that why you are here?

Believe it or not, this happens to people a lot and is a very common motivator for people to start thinking about writing a book.

I imagine you heard this and thought a couple things:

1. "A book? Yeah, right? I'm not a writer."

2. "A book? Really? People would want to read my story? How do I start? I'm not really a writer, but if it will help somebody, I'm willing to at least look into it."

Maybe you thought a mixture of the two above. And maybe you were led to this book because their words confirmed something you've known for a while now—you are called to write. You feel that burning fire to release something important that's been welling up inside of you.

Now let me offer this: when the passion to do something starts with you, that's usually where the gold is. Just because someone says you should do something does not mean you should. Write a book because you want to, because, I am telling you, the writing process is too wonderful and horrible a journey for it to be tied to someone else's fluctuating belief in you. You have to believe in yourself to make a book work—unrelentingly, audaciously believe.

Whatever your origin story is, you are here now excited to learn how to get those words on to paper and into readers' hands. Yes, you are really about to do this. Good for you! Now let me get you some answers, so you can start and finish well.

Chapter One: One Bite at a Time

The truth is, achieving the goal of becoming a published author is like the trick to eating an elephant: take one bite at a time. There is so much information about publishing this and book marketing that. But the first thing you need to do is having a writing plan. The plan I have outlined for many aspiring authors begins with the main thing—developing great content. That is the first at this stage.

When you are just deciding to write a book, you don't need to think about the book cover, who is going to review your book, or what shows you are going to get on. That will cause divided thinking and what you need at this stage is focus so that you are able to make the right decisions to build a solid foundation that future publishing opportunities will stand on.

Without being very sure of the following nine things, your book project will not go very far. This is my "first things first" plan to get you started:

1. Why are you writing a book?

There are other place for your story to appear—magazine articles, newspaper, local news story, blogs, testimony shared at church or another kind of meeting or gathering... You have to know for yourself why it should be a book. Also, consider the length for most books in the market is between 40,000 and 60,000 words. Will it take that many words to tell your story effectively and efficiently?

2. Whom are you writing for—specifically?

Everyone will not—cannot—benefit from your book. Think of this: who will want to read your book? Not, who needs to read your book? Some people, even if they need something, just will not be in the frame of mind to receive what they need. But there are those who really want something and they are willing to read a book to get it. Who is that person for the topic you want to write about? Identify them, then write to them.

3. What do you want to write about?

What is your main topic and goal for the book?

4. What will the reader gain from reading your book?

By the time they finish your book what will their lives be like, what will they be motivated to do, what will they have learned? What's in it for them? It is *hugely* important that you know this like the back of your hand or you won't be able to articulate the felt need—the reason why someone would want to read your book along with (or instead of) all the other millions that are written and published every year. This will be your so-called sales pitch and how you are able to draw a strong connection with your readers to see their lives impacted in some way by your message.

Note: Write out a combination of numbers 3 and 4 in a succinct paragraph of about 300 to 500 words. Have people read it who don't know your story—and maybe a just few who do? Get their feedback. You will need and should learn to value objective feedback. Some writers will consult with an editor or an agent friend at this point. It may cost you some to grab an hour of their time, but it is so very worth it. What you are developing and getting feedback on is your book summary or synopsis.

5. Should what you are aiming to write even be a book?

An editor or agent may be great to pull in on this step as well. Sometimes what you believe should be a whole book, may not be as substantial as you though and would work better as an article in a magazine, newspaper, or well-trafficked blog. Every story is not a book. Is there enough information to write a 50,000-word book that will hold your reader's interest from start to finish? Is it something people will pay money for?

If you can see yourself filling out at least 50,000 words on a given topic for an adult audience, continue to number 6. (We'll talk more about various word count requirements in a later chapter.)

6. Develop a chapter-by-chapter outline...

...with the above things in mind. The chapters should be based on the lessons, ideas, or concepts you want to support your main topic. Is it how to overcome depression? Then each chapter will need to highlight each step in the process or journey to overcoming depression.

7. Think of how you will illustrate each step, lesson, or concept.

Will you use an anecdote, a personal story, a graph, a chart, statistics, scientific research, a biblical illustration, a story in a famous or historical person's life?

8. Will you be using secondary sources...

...such as other books, magazine articles, websites, journal, encyclopedias, notes from a conference you attended? Make sure to cite them as endnotes or footnotes.

9. Make sure you have a compelling introduction and conclusion.

The introduction sets the tone for the whole book. In it you will outline why you are writing the book, the promise you are making to the reader of where they will end up after they have read the book, the steps they will go through to get there, and a motivating charge to them to keep reading. The conclusion wraps everything that was said in the book with a nice, little bow. It restates everything the reader read in a neat package. These are the takeaways. I recommend that it also includes a motivational charge for the reader to not just leave everything they learned in the book and close but to take what they have read and apply it to their lives to see some kind of lasting change or transformation.

There are other things you can include in a nonfiction book such as chapter quotes at the beginning of each chapter the supports the topic for that chapter (gives the reader a little nugget too. I like little nuggets, thoughts, or questions for reflection at the end of each chapter, also small group and interactive questions if your book would be good for a book club or Bible study group.

But even more than all of this is the amount of work you have to be willing to put in to writing your book. That is the hardest part. It is much easier, though, when you have a plan.

Let's now take a deeper look into some of the steps in the writing and publishing process I mention above.

Chapter Two: Who Are You Writing For?— Discovering Your Target Audience

> Successful authors understand that the focus must be put on the reader and satisfying the reader's needs. Even in the most personal writing, a memoir or autobiography, the writer shares her struggles and triumphs in an effort to help the reader make better sense of his own.
> —TODD SATTERSTEN, *EVERY BOOK IS A STARTUP* (O'REILLY, 2012)

Discovering your target audience is like the jelly part of a PB&J sandwich; the topic itself is totally the peanut butter. Those two elements need to be clearly defined before you put pen to paper.

Many times, when we discuss our writing projects, we verbally articulate who we are writing for, but when we take a closer look, sometimes it's hard to match whom we said we were writing for with the writing itself. I've seen this many times during the editing process and when I have reviewed manuscripts for publication. The query or the proposal will say one thing, because the author may understand what I am looking for, but when I actually read the piece, the focus is scattered. A similar thing happens when the author is not able to pointedly tell me who their audience is.

If you can't answer the question, Who are you writing this book for?, you will have a hard time putting together a well-formed piece that connects with readers. But no worries. Let's see if we can put our heads together and figure this thing out.

One of the things I do, even in editing, is google the topic I am working on and see who is saying what about it. Then I check out who seems to be reading and sharing what is written—retweeting it, facebooking it, whatever. I look at blog comments. I visit organization websites that provide similar resources or solves the problem I am writing about and see who attends their workshops or conferences. I look to see who they say they are providing their services for. Then I make a list of those people. I categorize them. I cross out the ones that don't exactly fit my core audience—or maybe I leave them as my secondary audience.

One of my mentors told me that once I discover the simplest composite of my audience, I need to narrow it down to one single person, find a suitable visual image, print it out, and tape it to my computer or somewhere in my eye's view while I write or edit. I thought this idea was genius. Do you do this?

You should know the basics of who you are writing for:

- Gender
- Ethnicity
- Age
- Education level
- Faith or religious preference
- Economic status
- Relationship status
- Occupation
- Common life situations; be specific (working moms, men with young children whose wives died young, over forty and unmarried, etc.)

You don't have to answer all of these for every project. These are examples of very important things to know about whom you are aiming your piece at. Knowing this information will build your sensitivity and will help as you choose words, pull together examples and illustrations, and form your arguments. (Side note: jargon and stilted language can actually work if the audience is right.) Being able to show that you were, at some point, where the reader is right now helps them to feel like they can relate to you —and in turn helps you sell books, builds your readers' confidence in you as a writer and authority on that particular topic, and sets a successful foundation for your next project.

Chapter Three: Organizing Your Book for Maximum Impact

While there is an overwhelming amount of unsalable personal testimonies or memoirs, the author submitting this kind of book could easily remedy that problem by revising their book and forming it into a how-to or self-help book based on principles they learned by overcoming the difficulties in their life.

The Introduction

You don't have to write a whole long piece on your life story right in the beginning, but just some bits and pieces about what caused you to write on a specific topic, why you are sharing it with the world, what you hope to see change as a result of your sharing, and how change can be brought about (e.g. "ten ways to improve your relationships," "thirty days to a new you," or "letting go of the past through forgiveness"). More of your story can be shared as little bite-size examples/anecdotes later in the book as it relates to the points or steps you identify to help the reader along the path you've outlined for them.

The Body

Most nonfiction books need to have a clear focus and road map from the beginning. Your chapters will flow out of that structure—each one building on the last and each one representing the rungs in the ladder for which you are leading the reader to climb.

For example, a book called *Ten Steps to True Happiness* could start with an intro for what happiness is, why you are writing about happiness, what incident in your life caused you to see the value of happiness, and what you see possible for people reaching the true happiness they deserve. Then each chapter following would discuss and highlight each step in how to obtain true happiness—and maybe with little short examples from your own life.

The Challenge, Charge, or Conclusion

Then you could conclude with a charge and motivation for the reader to maintain and continue to find ways to build happiness and maybe even share that happiness with others. I think it's cool to activate people into what they have just learned. Learning isn't powerful until you can apply it to change the world around you. Doesn't have to be big, but if you can give your readers a solid way to live out what you've just shared, then you know you have a winner and you wouldn't have survived the loss, failure, or experience you went through in vain.

This is a very simplified example, but many times, the manuscripts I review do not have even this kind of structure. New/first-time authors, you must understand that your thoughts need to be clear and organized so that the reader will feel safe and connected to you as you guide them down a well-lit road. At the most basic level, readers really like to have their information handed to them. Life is hard enough without having to search through a book to find the nuggets. Most likely, readers will not search.

Chapter Four: It's All About the Reader— Considerations While You Write

A good book is measured by the response it evokes from the reader. It captures the heart of the reader. The goal is to help the reader understand and stay connected by the consistency of the content (concept) of the book. Always think about the end result, and how is this book going to help the reader to grow, change, or see the Christian life from a different perspective. Ask yourself, "Is the reader being enlightened? What's the take away value? What's the WOW factor?"

Become part of the audience as you write. Would this book interest you, and, if so, will you learn something new? Will you grow in your walk and relationship with the Lord?

Unique and Different

Another very important thing to consider: is what you're writing about something that has already been said, and, if it is, what makes yours unique and different? What is the unique selling point? Are there other books similar to yours, and how does yours compare in terms of being different? Yet, even though similar content may be out there, the skill is to put a fresh spin or a new twist on the same topic, to make it relevant for today's reading audience, especially with the demographic of the readership changing.

Writing Life into Your Book

Find creative and compelling ways to add your or others' experiences to the content. This is the life of the book. Readers want something to connect with, and anecdotal stories help. These don't have to be in detail. Just let them be enough to keep the reader engaged. Weave them throughout the book. Anecdotal stories, or humor, must be in good taste. A splash of humor adds a bit of spice or flavor. Again, this must be in good taste.

Note that anecdotal material and biblical references should support the principle you are teaching about. In other words, the principle you are teaching about should be the main *character* in the chapter, and anecdotal and biblical references should be the *supporting cast*. The topic (theme) of your book should run through each chapter. Each chapter should have that theme as a thread that connects each chapter.

Consistency is very important. Each paragraph should have one topic as the focal point. And then, the wrap-up at the end of the book should drive home the topic (theme) of the book—how it all ties together.

Don't Overwhelm with Dry Facts and Data

While facts are good and needed, try not to have too much where the reader loses interest. The whole idea is to keep the reader engaged until the end of the book. The average reader has to be able to understand and grasp what's being written about. When writing, try including yourself as part of the audience. Again, ask yourself, "Does it help the reader tap divine resources? Do they sense the presence of God?"

What helps is to envision the reader in front of you as you write. Make the content clear, concise, and interesting. Write the way you talk but better.

Books that encourage the reader, books that help that person discover all God means to them, and books about how to overcome the problems of life are always good topics to deliver. They also allow you to easily develop and meet your author promise, which is what you promise the reader will gain by the time they reach at the end of the book.

Avoid Clique-ish Buzz Words, Clichés, and Slogans

The average reader does not understand "christianese," so avoid using Christian slogans, terminology, or Christian "buzz" words that the average reader would not understand. Every reader is at the different level of spiritual growth or maturity, so gear your writing toward the everyday reader.

For the most part, they are the ones who make up the readership. In the same way, avoid verbose words, or words that one would have to look up the meaning to—unless it's a book being written for scholars.

Write Fresh for Today

As you have defined the market (the audience) for your book, make the material applicable to today's readers. The culture today is very different from yesteryear, so it is important to know or describe the readership for your material. Keep in mind the reading audience is also very different. The publishing landscape has changed tremendously from what it was even ten years ago, so books have to be relevant, fresh, and captivating.

Write It. Forget It. Rewrite It.

A side note: it's been said and is good advice to write the book (article, poem, song etc.), leave it alone for a few days, then go back and rewrite it. Usually what happens, is that you see things that you did not see before. Go back and rearrange sections, paragraphs, and so on, so that your words and message flow better. It takes a lot of patience to write something that will change lives and impact the world around you.

Chapter Five: Writing to Felt Need vs. Real Need

Not so long ago, I was working with an author who has a huge platform but was having trouble connecting the messages in their books with their core audience. It would seem easy since what they present to the world is appealing to a large group of people, but it's not always easy to translate a public persona into a compelling concept.

The gap between how a message is presented live and in person and how it is written and experienced in a book is a common challenge for many authors, especially nonfiction authors. Being able to identify the difference between real needs and felt needs can mean the difference between a good book and a great book.

One way to overcome this is to know why your core audience engages with you.

Why do they follow you? The reason they follow you is because you are meeting a felt need of theirs. Identify those needs, then build your book projects around them.

Here's how I define felt needs and real needs in this context:

- Felt needs can be simplified to being synonymous to wants, wishes, hopes, and, in short to issues, changes, results a person deems necessary for their lives.

- Real needs often refer to the real qualities and efforts a person needs to develop or utilize that lead to the results they desire.

Here are some examples.

Real Needs an author may want to write about	Felt Needs a reader may want help with
Humility	Success, greatness, notoriety
Exercise and eat right every day	Eat what I want, lose weight fast, look young forever
Generosity	Abundance, wealth
Strong spiritual relationship with God, consistent prayer life, obedience, submission to God's will over yours	Miracles, breakthrough, healing, prosperity
Strong work ethic and high integrity to see some success, rise and grind	Work as little as possible, get big and lasting results/returns
Love is a choice, love is work, expect to give more than you get, you can't change the other person	Feeling in love all the time, he/she just gets me, ten steps to staying in love every day
Heal the world, end hunger and poverty, world peace	Heal me and my family, feeding me and my family, bring peace to me and my family

You may be thinking both sets of needs appear to be real. It's true. Both felt and real needs are legitimate. But sometimes as people of great passion and conviction, authors have arrived at places in their own lives where they've come to see larger issues that are affecting groups of people versus individual lives. I think it's noble for authors to help readers rise above their circumstances and answer to higher callings and the like. But it's all about how you lead them to do this.

It's likely that you see people's real needs and just want to help them with the real solution, so you dive in, tackling their issues head on—like giving them medicine without a spoonful of sugar. But what you'll notice, if you release a concept like this, your audience generally will reject real-needs messages as quickly and strongly as they will receive felt-needs messages. Just compare your social media posts: which ones get the most responses, likes, or shares?

My recommendation: address felt need up front and just kind of slide the medicine, the behavior and habit changes (the real need), in there, in between.

You may think that handling your message in this way waters it down, but I strongly disagree. Carefully planning how to present your message shows that you understand what it takes for your readers to get from point A to point B. The sense that you get them will translate and will cause your message to get into more hands, affecting a larger audience than it would if you went right into what you see as your readers' real need.

When you show that you can relate, you are not watering anything down. You are actually revealing your own humanity. If your purpose is to empower, inspire, or teach, you must get on eye level first. It's basic empathy. Then they will be open to receiving from you what they need to not only get there (felt need) but also to receiving what they need to stay there (real need). Does that make sense?

As you develop your concepts, consider what your goals are for the project. You don't have to have a grandiose vision, but you will feel accomplished and satisfied when your book project releases and meets your set expectations.

If this continues to be a challenge for you, consider consulting with an industry-experienced editor, one who has experience working on books that compare to yours.

They can help you home in on the felt needs of your audience and help you develop books that center on those needs.

Chapter Six: What Is the Right Word Count for Your Book?

Here is my quick-reference guide to common word count ranges so you can know what to aim for depending on the genre you are writing in.

Ebook-only Promo

I may have made up this category, but I believe every up-and-coming expert-author-person should seriously consider having one of these. They are great little books to use for platform-building, for giveaways on your website to grow your mailing list, to pitch yourself for speaking engagements, or other special promos or opportunities. Their word count should be bite-size at

2,500–10,000 words

Booklets

10,000–15,000 words

General Nonfiction

50,000–70,000 words

Some titles come in at 25,000–40,000 words and make powerful purse-size resources. Think *Who Moved My Cheese*, *The Art of War*, *The Prayer of Jabez*, and *Prayers That Rout Demons*.

Fiction and Memoir

70,000–90,000 words

Novellas

50,000-60,000 words

Children's and
Young Adult (YA) Fiction

Middle grade: 20,000–55,000 words

YA: 55,000–80,000 words

Easy/early readers: 2,000–5,000 words

Chapter books: 2,500–10,000 words

Picture books: 500–1,000 words

***

Some first-time authors have mentioned to me that they want to write small books of less than five thousand to ten thousand words, some less, because they don't want to give their readers too much to read. Don't be afraid to write within the word count ranges I listed above. They're the standard for what people have been reading for centuries. You read books of this length all the time without flinching, and if you make it good, your readers will want to read this much from you.

Also, consider that if you want to catch the attention of agents or publishers, they pay attention to these word count ranges, and it's cool if you show some savvy about the industry by giving them and your readers what they expect.

On Word Counts for First-Time Authors

For some time now in coaching sessions with brand-new authors, I've noticed a good majority of them telling me that they are writing a small book—many times less than five thousand words—because they believe that people do not want to read full-length books. They don't want to burden the reader with too many words.

My first thought toward this is, I wonder if new authors are aware that the most common word count for a nonfiction book is about fifty thousand words. People read these books at these lengths—like 76 percent of those who purchase these books. (See Pew Research article, "Who Doesn't Read Books in America?") So, I had been curious where the new authors I was coaching came to understand that very small books are the way to go for a first book. It's just not a right conclusion. A few publishing friends chimed in to contribute their thoughts on this. I'll add them at the end of this chapter.

For discussion's sake, five thousand words would yield a book of about twenty printed pages or so depending on font size and other things. Most books we see at the bookstore are about two hundred pages. However, an ebook at five thousand words or less could work really well for a specific purpose. (That's a whole other strategy session.)

The other thing I am thinking is that aspiring authors are not just misinformed but perhaps their knowledge is lacking in what actual word count ranges are of even their favorite books. I pray they are reading books like the ones they hope to write. Most are writing memoirs. I hope they are reading good ones—Maya Angelou, Anna LeBaron, Michelle Obama, and others. And maybe being new at book writing, they are surrounded by nonreaders and are getting feedback on how long their book should be from people who don't like to read.

Here are more of my thoughts on this as someone from the inside communicating out:

1. Write a book people will read. Make it great, and word count may not matter so much in indie publishing (publishers have stricter word count guidelines). People will keep reading as long as they feel a need to—and that

need is "felt need." If a book is not engaging, if it is not scratching an itch, if it is not answering the reader's unspoken question of "What's in it for me?" they won't read it regardless of the word count.

2. Word count ranges are not arbitrary. Studies on reader behavior—what people read, how much they read, how much they spend on a book, what mediums they use to read, where they shop, and so on—are readily available. So the word count numbers for various genres, price points, etc. are not made up out of the blue. Then there so many words needed to fully develop a story, point, or method so the book's promise is satisfied. As an

aspiring author, it is good to start writing from an informed position. Here's one study from Pew Research Center: https://www.pewinternet.org/2016/09/01/book-reading-2016/. This research group does these kinds of studies periodically.

3. Refer back to my QUICK-REFERENCE GUIDE TO COMMON WORD COUNT RANGES at the beginning of this chapter.

4. You can break the rules and be intentionally different. Why care about the market? You don't necessarily have to do all the market dictates, but we live in an economy that is driven by supply and demand. You want to be in demand, yes? Then you need

to know the market. You can't dominate or master what you don't understand. Though there are some really cool anomalies, runaway hits and such, that no one can make sense of. There are also variables that consistently produce the same successful results over time that yield proven methods and highlight factors one needs to have in order to be in demand. Those factors have been studied for a long time and are available to us to leverage for our own products and outputs. We don't have to always follow them. We can be innovative. But it is at least good to know the rules so when you set out to break, you break

them well, on purpose, and
with intention.

Here's what a few of my colleagues had
to say about why first-time authors want to
write such small books:

> They are not readers. Readers know
> what is being published. Like many
> writers publishing "novels" in
> ebook format are really publishing
> either novellas or short, category
> length novels. Not as many are
> writing 80K plus books once they
> explore self-publishing. This is fine
> but when readers get a 25–35K
> "novel," they sometimes feel
> cheated. Because readers know.
> —PATRICIA W., FREELANCE EDITOR
> AND BOOK REVIEWER

1. Writers have read such books by
authors such as Mike Murdock, not
realizing those were self-pubbed.

2. Writers don't realize every idea
can't easily be developed into a full-

length book because idea is too narrow and perhaps should be an article.

3. Some writers want the "fame" of writing a book, but wisely understand writing a "big" book takes a lot of time and effort.

4. Some writers don't read, so they have no idea of length. For example, people who don't read books for children so they think 5,000+ words is a good picture book length.

—LISA C., WRITER, WRITING COACH, SPEAKER, WORKSHOP FACILITATOR

My response to Lisa's feedback:

In response to your point #1, an author recently sent me a book as an example for how they wanted their book designed. When I received the book, I realized it was self-published and did not follow a typical traditionally published format. The author had no idea. So I can see what you mean here.

I also see that people follow patterns of their favorite authors who may have strong platforms that support their unconventional publishing patterns. A new author may not have the clout or respect built up just yet to pull off some of the things we see well-established authors do—OUTSIDE their traditional publishing strategies, mind you. I don't even think there's an awareness that there are two worlds--traditional and independent —colliding in one platform with some of the more prominent authors.

Though it is highly recommended that you do not get caught up on how many words you are writing, especially during your first draft, it is something that should be in your mind as you plan your book's content.

Chapter Seven: Getting to the Right Word Count

Are you working toward a word count and it seems like an impossible goal because you are running out of things to say or you've let your wordiness get the best of you and now you've said too much? Well, let me help you. I have been known to take an author's manuscript that was half the word count it was supposed to be and double it or reduced what seemed impossible to condense. Without watering down the content by stretching too much or cutting out critical parts, these cool tricks will help you get your word count just right.

How to Lengthen Your Nonfiction Book When You Feel Like You've Said Everything

Job number-one: review what you have written. Then ask yourself these five questions (oh and answer them):

1. Is there a step in my process for which I need to offer more explanation to the reader?

It's good to ask yourself as you are writing, "If I were a novice, would I really understand what I have written here?" Make sure that you are writing to the level of understanding of your target audience. Don't know who your target audience is? Go to https://www.jevonbolden.com/2012/02/who-are-you-writing-for-discovering.html, read, and then come back.

2. Could a story, testimony, or example add more impact, interest, or understanding to any of my points?

People like to see how a process or bit of advice worked out for someone in a real and relatable situation. Maybe you could have done that for a few of your points to really have your concept hit home. If so, do it and add more words.

3. Is it clear to my readers why what I have written matters?

If yes, do not write more on that. If no, write more in the introduction or first chapter about why what you are writing is important for your readers and to you. Do not overstate this.

4. Could I interject more whys into the rest of the book?

Making sure the reader can follow the context for each point you make may be helpful. Do this so that you are not creating a because-I-said-so scenario. This also helps with continuity, flow, and tie-in for the main topic of your book.

5. Is there more research or additional expertise from secondary sources I can cite and include?

Not only does this add further credibility to your work, but it also gives the reader the feeling that they are in a room full of smart people to help them through their journey—whatever it is. Now listen, let the bulk of what you deliver in your book be you. Do not go ham on the secondary sources. Readers buy your book to hear from you.

Finally here are some other ways you can stretch the content of your manuscript:

- Choose dynamic pull quotes.

- Add helpful sidebars (e.g., ten foods that help boost your metabolism, top ten apps for working moms).

- Tack on discussion questions or points to ponder at the end of each chapter.

- Pull in additional front or back matter such as a foreword, preface, introduction, conclusion, epilogue, or resource page.

- Include appropriate visual aids such as illustrations, graphs, or charts. (No clip art!)

How to Shorten Your Nonfiction Book When You Feel Like You Couldn't Have Said Less

Are you at a point in writing your book where the 100,000-word mark is a distant memory? Is your book so long that Jesus may come before anybody can finish reading it? And maybe you've been writing on your book for years and have no idea what the word count is or how to find out. I think that perhaps now is the time to click the Tools menu in Word, select Word Count, and see where you are.

As I pointed out in the last chapter, the standard word count on a typical nonfiction trade book is between 40,000 and 60,000 words. Have you written much more than this? Well, I have been known to take 100,000-word books and cut them down to 60,000 words without affecting the punch, author voice, or quality of information it contains. So let me help you meet your goal of writing a concise, well-developed nonfiction book that will keep your readers' interest and give them just the right amount of content they need to take what you have to offer and build on it themselves for their own lives.

First you will need to carefully review what you have written, chapter by chapter and point by point. Sometimes it helps to outline the book again listing each story, illustration, example, or research supporting your main points. Once you've done this, you need to ask yourself these questions:

Have I offered too much detail in expressing my points?

In other words, is there a point the reader may say, "I go it. Enough already! Geez!"? Sometimes you are saying more than you need to say. Have someone read portions of your manuscript with you for an objective perspective. Then mark places where you can thin those explanations out.

Are there certain points in my book that could do without the additional stories, examples, or personal testimonies?

Sometimes in nonfiction you can get away with telling and not showing— sometimes. I often cut the illustrative stories and just leave the author's points to stand on their own when I am trying to decrease word count.

Have I gone on too many tangents or rabbit trails?

Some ways this can be evident is you catch yourself saying, "...so back to what I was saying..." or "Let's get back to the main point." You went off on a side thought, entertained it too long, and got off course. Cut some of that out. Snip, snip!

Have I said things over and over? Are there places where I am restating things that have already been made clear enough in other places in the manuscript?

This is called redundancy. When you are reading someone else's book, it would cause you to say to them, "You said that already, man!" Make sure you are not beating a dead horse. This can happen very easily when you are passionate about something. Harness your passion, say precisely what you mean to say, and move on.

Do I have too many sources quoted or are the quotes too long?

While sourcing other authorities can help strengthen your credibility on a topic, sometimes there can just be too much from other sources that crowd your original thoughts. If you find yourself at war with meeting a certain word count, look at what you can cut from the secondary sources. Direct quotes are what I go after first here, then I see what studies or set of statistics I can cut that were really only loosely supporting the main point. There are some occasions that this kind of secondary sourcing is crucial, but you may find places in your book where they are not. Cut 'em!

Other things you can do to shorten your book:

- Delete sidebars and other add-ons that are not essential.

- Determine what from the front and back matter can be cut:

preface, acknowledgments, epilogue, conclusion, resources pages, appendixes. Information from resource pages and appendixes can be included on your website as reader perks and helps.

- Cut chapter opening quotes

- If you were including questions at the end of each chapter, pull those out and make a digital study guide or workbook that can be a free download for people who join your email list or subscribe to your blog.

If you find difficulty seeing how to make these changes yourself, then it is time to reach out to a developmental editor who can offer a manuscript critique. Their critique can give you clear steps on how to get your book on the right track. If it's even too much from there, considering hiring the editor to do all the changes for you. You are not alone in your writing process. Help is available for just about anything you need.

There! Now that should do it.

Chapter Eight: The Components of a Completed Manuscript?

The information in this chapter may not apply to you if you are being well-coached or your publishing process is being managed by a fantastic agent, who will make sure that everything on my list below is ready and presented at the time of initial query. But for this will help you if you are publishing independently.

If you are working with a traditional publisher, this information applies to the stage between contract and submission of your final manuscript. When I was an in-house editor for traditional publishers, what I would find is many times I would receive a manuscript from an author that is missing quite a few vital components. These components should be part of the writing phase as you prepare your manuscript for publication.

This list also comes in handy for authors who are self-publishing and are ready to acquire the services of an editor.

In either case, you don't want your editor to have to go hunting for all this info if you are able to give it to them up front. This will your editor to spend as much quality time with your content as the editorial schedule will allow—and you want that. An editor is an expert at making sure the author is all neat and tucked in, but should they also be responsible for doing things the author should have prepared beforehand?

Yes, everyone should play their parts well.

So here's a checklist of items and tasks that need to be completed before an author submits their final manuscript to their publisher or their freelance editor. Not all of these elements will apply to all projects.

Here's what you need to turn in *with* your manuscript:

- Endorsements
- Dedication
- Acknowledgments
- Foreword
- Preface
- Prologue
- Introduction
- Table of contents
- List of tables, charts, graphs, or images
- Charts/tables
- Graphs
- Photographs, graphics, or other images
- Print licenses for song or poetry lyrics; long quotes from books, websites, and news

articles; use of charts, graphs, or photographs; or any other copyrighted material

- Full sourcing (or citation) information for all borrowed and quoted material including author, title, publisher's city and state, publisher's name, publishing date, page number, and/or web link

- Signed releases from subjects mentioned by
name or likeness in your book (changing a subject's name is not enough)

- Conclusion

- Epilogue

- Appendices

- Bibliography

- Endnotes or footnotes

- Index list

- About the author page

If you are at this stage (between contract and final manuscript or just about ready to turn your manuscript over to your editor), print this list and put it up in your writing station.

Many times, and maybe other editors can relate, chasing down and completing this information impose on my edit time—especially signed releases, print licenses, and sourcing. While editors typically love the thrill of a chase, their time could be better spent really homing in on your message or story and helping to make it shiny and life-changing for your readers. It's for the readers that publishers and authors do any of it, right?

Chapter Nine: Media Law 101—What You Need to Know about Libel and Defamation[1]

We are living in a fairly litigious culture, where people take each other to court for various reasons. One common reason for having a claim filed in book publishing is violation of a person's privacy or saying cruel or untrue things about them. With most first-time authors writing their personal stories of trauma, abuse, spiritual awakening, or coming of age, there is a high-risk for violating the rights of those who interacting with their stories in various ways and at various times.

---

[1] *The definitions and terms in this chapter are adapted from handouts from a Media Law Seminar conducted at Charisma Media on January 19, 1999 by Allen, Dyer, Doppelt, Milbrath & Gilchrist, PA.*

Accusations of libel or defamation that precede lawsuits can be challenging ordeals most authors can avoid, and I want to help you do that. I'll start by defining libel, defamation law, and right of privacy. Then I'll talk about ways you can protect yourself and respect the rights of those whose names or images you would like to include in your fiction or nonfiction piece.

The Basics

Libel involves the publication of written defamatory material, or a defamatory statement recorded in some other permanent form (such as videotape or film). It can occur through the use of an inaccurate quotation, a miscaptioned photograph, or the omission of pertinent facts. Both fiction and nonfiction works can be defamatory.

A *defamatory statement* is a false statement of fact that injures or harms the reputation of a living person or an existing business. You cannot libel someone who is dead. The statement must have been published, and read or heard by someone other than the person who was defamed. Because of the First Amendment and the fact that defamation law is a state law, the tests for liability depends on whether the person suing is a public official or a celebrity or just a private person, or whether the defamatory statement concerns a matter of public or private interest.

The injured person must establish all of the following to be true:

1. The statement made about them was false. This is not so cut and dry and can be all about interpretation.

2. The statement had a defamatory meaning— injuring reputation; impeaching honesty, integrity, and sanity; or

affecting a person's political office, profession, business, or ownership or interest in land or real estate

3. The statement clearly pointed to their person or identity by name or likeness.

4. The statement was published.

5. The statement caused damage to the person's reputation.

6. The person who wrote the statement is indeed at fault.

In certain circumstances the injured person must also prove economic harm—loss of wages or opportunity.

The *right of privacy* protects a person's peace of mind, sensibilities, and feelings. So it goes beyond what even defamation law protects, which is truth and reputation. People have a legal right to be free from unwarranted and unauthorized exposure of his or her person, or those personal affairs in which the public has no legitimate interest. In others words, we all have a right to be left alone.

A person's privacy can be violated in four ways:

1. Physical intrusion

2. Disclosure of private facts

3. Publicizing them in a false light

4. Misappropriating the use of his or her name or likeness for commercial purposes

Minimizing Your Liability

Here are some ways to minimize libel claims:

1. Double check the accuracy of all statements about any

living person, business entity, or product.

2. Keep detailed logs of calls and contacts made during the fact-checking process, and take outstanding notes documenting what you have done (including your failed attempts to reach people).

3. Obtain written releases whenever possible.

4. Recognize the people who are most likely to sue: doctors, lawyers, chiropractors, accountants, public figures, religious figures, educators, business executives, even figures who are not central to the main story but are shown in an unflattering light

5. Watch out for red-flag statements that imply that a person committed a crime,

acted irrationally or
unethically, was incompetent,
is financially irresponsible,
acted in a heretical manner,
or is involved with a
disreputable organization.

6. Use criminal law terminology
   accurately.

7. If your story is partially or
   wholly fictional, but based on
   real people, change the
   names, places, and
   identifying information
   sufficiently so that no live
   person can be identified. And
   don't use the names of other
   real people.

8. Review the entire manuscript
   —including preface, forward,
   captions, and illustrations—
   prior to publication.

9. Organize your research and
   be certain that all factual

statements can be verified by adequate evidence.

A person (author, journalist, publisher, etc.) can defend against invasion of privacy accusations by proving

1. They had the subject's consent.

   The shared information was public information.

2. The shared information was newsworthy and of public interest. (Note that this defense may weaken over time, because information that was once of public concern can become private with the passage of time.)

3. The shared information was from court records.

4. The shared information was about a deceased person

(which does not hold up in
some states like Florida).

5. The shared information was
not offensive, which could be
arguable.

Not every detail or nuance to these
laws are covered in this chapter, but it should
get you headed in the right direction. Realize
that all of these things have to be proven and
defended and then interpreted and decided
by a judge. Also know that while you think
something isn't a big deal, a claim can be filed
against you. You may not be proven guilty,
but it also works to avoid these circumstances
if you can.

Study up on this topic if you are writing
a memoir, autobiography, or nonfiction book
with personal accounts in them. It will be
worth your time.

I am not a lawyer, but I do recommend
that you work closely with one to help you

sort out your individual concerns or issues. Your editor should also have an excellent working knowledge of media law and may be able to provide you with great advice and counsel.

Chapter Ten: Teamwork Makes the Dream Work— Key Players for Your Publishing Dream Team

Being in the publishing business for fifteen years has afforded me the opportunity to be on some of the best and brightest publishing teams in the industry—*New York Times*–bestseller, award-winning marketing and sales people, award-winning graphic designers, and simply the best writing and editing people around. Needless to say, my network for help and support when I need it in my own venture at jevonbolden.com runs deep. You can see some of the projects my dream team has accomplished here: https://embolden mediagroup.com/projects.

But what's great about how the publishing industry is opening up, you can have your own publishing dream team as well.

All you need to know are the list of players to recruit, where to find them, and what are the resources you need to pull out their best creative work. If want to publish an industry-competitive book without the industry restrictions, here are the independent publishing professionals you'll need on your team to pull it off.

Project Manager

This well-connected individual should know how to pull together a team and lead them to a completed project. They should be familiar with the publishing process and fabulous at communicating to all parties involved. This person may double as your ghostwriter or editor, depending on their skills.

Ghostwriter

A gifted, industry-savvy, trends-aware writer who knows how to keep your voice and message ahead of their own, ghostwriters love the background and want to make you shine. Get a list of their previous projects, personal reading and writing interests, educational background, and their writing style and preferences for how they work with authors.

Content Editor

A gifted, industry-savvy, trends-aware editor who's been in the publishing industry and knows how to cultivate great content, your editor ought to be able to help you hone your message to a specific yet broad target audience. They should know *Chicago Manual of Style* (CMOS) like the back of their hand—or at least how to find what they need to get your book tight. More than that, though, they are big-picture thinkers and can really give you specific content fixes and guidance that really enhances the quality and reach of your book. Don't use this type of editor for just grammar. Get them to really help you craft a compelling narrative or message.

Copyeditor

This is whom you use for grammar and style—and they must indeed know the most recent version of the *Chicago Manual of Style* (CMOS) like the back of their hand. The fine details such as—commas vs. semicolons, if "4th" should be "fourth" or not—in your manuscript is this editor domain of passion. They should absolutely love finding the dangling participles and connecting them to their subjects. However, this editor should be comfortable with nuance—careful to not overcorrect to the point where you no longer sound like you.

Typesetter

These amazing professionals are your unsung heroes. They take your manuscript from a Word document and set it into a template in Adobe InDesign, which becomes a file the printers use to print your book. They will also help you with getting your book formatted and linked for ebook platforms. They make the interior of your book look like the interior of the next best-seller.

Proofreader

These pros come in after your book has been typeset (sometimes called galleys, galley proofs, or first pages). They read through your manuscript and check for typos, misspellings, minor punctuation issues, various typesetting issues, consistency on headers and footers, pagination, and any other details that may have been missed at the copyediting stage or that have arisen during typesetting. They should have an incredibly sharp and knowledgeable eye.

Graphic Designer

A master at digital visual design. They should be masters at the newest version of Adobe Creative Suite, especially InDesign and Photoshop. They should be able to capture the essence of your design and push it a bit to coincide with what's hot in the industry. This person should be able to show you book covers and marketing pieces that have helped launch or support authors or personalities whose look and style resonate with yours.

Branding/Marketing Consultant

Overall brand and marketing strategist to help build your platform and boost your visibility. You'll want to know that this person has led successful book marketing/author branding campaigns. They should have success stories to share. The following two dream team members sometimes come along with the marketing consultant.

Publicist

They will prepare press releases, media contacts, and various other notifications to get the word about you and your projects. They may also assist with getting you connected with book reviewers and bloggers, conference coordinators for speaking engagements, bookstore owners for signings, radio and TV show hosts for interviews.

Social Media Manager

These savvy individuals help busy movers and shakers like you stay active and engaged on social media, while you are busy doing your author thing. They will ghost tweet, write blogs and Facebook posts, post images and updates to Instagram, and more.

Web Designer

Mastering both graphic design and computer coding and programming, a web designer will create the look, layout, and features of your website. Some will even help you maintain it and keep the content fresh and updated. They should be willing to hear your needs as well as make professional and proven recommendations for your website to get the views, clicks, and buys that help support your budding platform.

Photographer

Having a photographer on speed dial (is this still a thing? I never used it) is so important in this hypervisual times. They will help you with photo shoots for headshots for digital and print media opportunities, your website, Instagram and other photo-driven social media; live action shots of you and your audience while you speak or present; photographing your products and other ancillary materials for various digital and print promotions.

Videographer

A videographer provides help with book trailers, YouTube videos, promo videos, and record and can curate and edit footage from speaking engagements and special appearances to make an exciting highlight reel.

Print Buyer

To get the best printing rates, some authors will get the help of a print buyer who knows the printing and manufacturing industry like the back of their hands. They should have a list of printers with whom they can negotiate price, printing dates, and delivery options all in your wallet's best interest. Print buyers are especially helpful when you are publishing a nontraditional book package—for example, a specialty journal with a padded cover, gilded edges, and ribbon marker.

Sales/Distribution

Sometimes this is built-in to the printing service you use, such as IngramSpark. But if you choose to go completely indie and want to choose the printer (as referenced above) and choose the stores you want your book to be sold in, the experts in this field have the contacts to help get your book in online and brick-and-mortar stores.

***

If all this work turns into you a publisher taking notice of you, your, platform, or your book, here's the team you may need:

Literary Agent

They will advise you on how to put together a compelling book concept and a stunning book proposal. Then they will present that book proposal to traditional book publishers, negotiate the terms of your publishing contract in your favor, and help you understand your contract. They may even offer tips on how to build your platform, and depending on how connected they are can help you make media connections, book speaking engagements, and other things that help propel your platform. They usually do not ask for any money up front, but they will require a percentage of your advance and royalties upon your getting signed to a publisher.

Intellectual Property Attorney

When you only need help with understanding and negotiating a contract, these are your go-to professionals. They can also help you unravel contractual disagreements with publishers once you are under contract. They can advise you on how to navigate copyright, libel, trademarks, and other issues pertaining intellectual property.

***

Now that you know that you know the people who make book publishing happen, you could totally do this thing on your own. Am I right? Really, though, that is your call. There are so many ways to reach your goals, and it won't always look like the next person's way. But know this:

> If you want to go fast, go alone. If you want to go far, go together.
> —An African proverb

And, I know you saw it coming a mile away, but it's true:

TEAMWORK MAKES THE DREAM WORK.

Chapter Eleven: Counting the Costs— Investing in Your Publishing Dreams

With every opportunity, there is a cost of participation. With every pursuit of an idea, there is a necessary withdrawal of resources. A very wise Man once said,

> For which of you, intending to build a tower, does not sit down first and count the cost, whether he has enough to finish it.
>
> —LUKE 14:23

You are at a place now that you have finished writing your book. Your heart's passion or life message is down on paper—all 100,000 words. LOL! I hope not that many. But however many words you penned, you've *finally* completed the task that almost killed you. Yes, I am very aware of how deep and heart wrenching the writing process can be. But no use crying over that. It's now time to cross the finish line with this thing.

What I have come to realize is that many independent authors don't fully consider how much money they need to budget to get a very nice, polished book product to properly represent them and their message. Authors have told me that they wrote their book to add to their credibility or because people who hear about their life story want it in book form because of how they were inspired. If this is the case it is important that the author develop a financial picture for what it will take to meet the demand of their readers and their career or professional aspirations.

Now, as I approach this topic, please know that I know there is more than one way to accomplish this task. What I am sharing with you is based on my fifteen years of experience working in both the traditional trade book industry as well as working with and advising independent authors. It is also based on common rates most freelancers charge as compiled by the Freelance Editor's Association: https://www.the-efa.org/rates. What I am going to give here is a basic list of the steps you should consider taking when working to get your book written, edited, and published as well as approximate costs for each step. I believe this will give you an idea of what to expect from the beginning and will help you navigate the best and most financially appropriate direction for publishing your book.

Again, this is not the bible; it is only a guide.

Potential Costs for Self-Publishing

1. Developmental editing (comes before writing in some cases

and includes developing the theme, target audience, tone, outline, chapter organization, etc.; may also include substantive editing) - from $3500

2. Substantive/content editing/ book doctoring - from $2500

3. Copyediting/line editing - from $1000

4. Typesetting/page layout - from $2 per page (250 words per page; average book is 240 pages)

5. Proofreading - from $500

6. Book cover design - from $300

7. Printing costs - varies

8. File conversion and upload fees for ebook - varies

Approximate total cost to publish a quality book $5,000–$10,000 plus printing and ebook conversion costs.

After they finish writing their book, most authors start at step 3 but really need to start at least at step 2. My recommendation would be to start at step one and see if you can skip to step 3 and go on from there. Getting advice from an industry professional before you spend all your sweat and tears on writing a book may save you a lot of rewriting and adjusting after the fact. I wouldn't ever recommend starting at step 5 after just completing the writing for your book.

Marketing and promotions may be another line item to add to the above list. I posted a simple and free social media marketing plan you can customize for your purposes that may suffice: https://www.jevonbolden.com/blog//2011/01/simple-no-cost-social-media-marketing.html. Also for a description of the levels of editing I talk about above, you can visit https://www.jevonbolden.com/services/#levels-of-editing.

Ghostwriting is another option for those who have a book idea but are honest enough to know they don't have the chops or the time to write their own book. This is a very respectable option. It is not cheating or lying. Ghostwriting is a bona fide skill and profession, and many ghostwriters are phenomenally talented and gifted at making others' ideas and concepts shine. The cost for ghostwriting can start as low as $5,000.

Listen, this is your baby. Taking the time to carefully weigh the cost to see it grow into something you will be proud of is just simply good parenting. I hope this list gives you some beginning steps as you plan to reach your goals and realize your dreams of becoming a successful published author.

Appendix: Book Ideas Log

This Book Ideas Log is a starting place for you to keep track of the best ideas you receive during your writing practice. You can write directly on these pages.

Here, you will have a place to create many outlines for the books you will write and you will have the beginnings of what's needed for a great book proposal.

Most good things start with a good plan, counting the costs, and measuring resources. Here's a tool that will help you lay the foundation for much of your future writings.

New Book Idea #1

Book Title

_____

Subtitle

_____

_____

Hook (a short, compelling statement that will grab the attention of your readers, an agent, or a publisher in 50 words or less)

_____

_____

_____

_____

Summary (250 words that tell what your
book is about and how readers will benefit
from reading it)

_____

_____

_____

_____

_____

_____

_____

_____

Target Audience (Names a specific type of
person—the person to whom you are called,
perhaps—who will be helped, encouraged,
entertained, taught, or motivated from
reading this book. "This book is for

everyone" is not the answer to this one, as you know you are not called to minister to everyone. To whom is this book sent? "This book will appeal to readers who want to heal from the pain of their past and live in peace and freedom" is an example of a good start to defining of your target audience.)

_____

_____

_____

_____

Chapter Title and Topic Ideas

Introduction (Title):

_____

What's it about?

_____

_____

_____

_____

_____

Chapter 2 (Title):

_____

What's it about?

_____

_____

_____

_____

_____

Chapter 3 (Title):

_____

What's it about?

_____

_____

_____

_____

_____

Chapter 4 (Title):

_____

What's it about?

_____

_____

_____

_____

_____

Chapter 5 (Title):

_____

What's it about?

_____

_____

_____

_____

_____

Chapter 6 (Title):

_____

What's it about?

_____

_____

_____

_____

_____

Chapter 7 (Title):

_____

What's it about?

_____

_____

_____

_____

_____

Chapter 8 (Title):

_____

What's it about?

_____

_____

_____

_____

_____

Chapter 9 (Title):

_____

What's it about?

_____

_____

_____

_____

_____

Chapter 10 (Title):

_____

What's it about?

_____

_____

_____

_____

_____

New Book Idea #2

Book Title

_____

Subtitle

_____

_____

Hook (a short, compelling statement that will grab the attention of your readers, an agent, or a publisher in 50 words or less)

_____

_____

_____

_____

Summary (250 words that tell what your book is about and how readers will benefit from reading it)

_____

_____

_____

_____

_____

_____

_____

_____

Target Audience (Names a specific type of person—the person to whom you are called, perhaps—who will be helped, encouraged, entertained, taught, or motivated from reading this book. "This book is for

everyone" is not the answer to this one, as you know you are not called to minister to everyone. To whom is this book sent? "This book will appeal to readers who want to heal from the pain of their past and live in peace and freedom" is an example of a good start to defining of your target audience.)

_____

_____

_____

_____

Chapter Title and Topic Ideas

Introduction (Title):

_____

What's it about?

_____

_____

_____

_____

_____

Chapter 2 (Title):

_____

What's it about?

_____

_____

_____

_____

_____

Chapter 3 (Title):

_____

What's it about?

_____

_____

_____

_____

_____

Chapter 4 (Title):

_____

What's it about?

_____

_____

_____

_____

_____

Chapter 5 (Title):

_____

What's it about?

_____

_____

_____

_____

_____

Chapter 6 (Title):

_____

What's it about?

_____

_____

_____

_____

_____

Chapter 7 (Title):

_____

What's it about?

_____

_____

_____

_____

_____

Chapter 8 (Title):

_____

What's it about?

_____

_____

_____

_____

_____

Chapter 9 (Title):

_____

What's it about?

_____

_____

_____

_____

_____

Chapter 10 (Title):

_____

What's it about?

_____

_____

_____

_____

_____

New Book Idea #3

Book Title

_____

Subtitle

_____

_____

Hook (a short, compelling statement that will grab the attention of your readers, an agent, or a publisher in 50 words or less)

_____

_____

_____

_____

Summary (250 words that tell what your book is about and how readers will benefit from reading it)

_____

_____

_____

_____

_____

_____

_____

_____

Target Audience (Names a specific type of person—the person to whom you are called, perhaps—who will be helped, encouraged, entertained, taught, or motivated from reading this book. "This book is for

everyone" is not the answer to this one, as you know you are not called to minister to everyone. To whom is this book sent? "This book will appeal to readers who want to heal from the pain of their past and live in peace and freedom" is an example of a good start to defining of your target audience.)

_____

_____

_____

_____

Chapter Title and Topic Ideas

Introduction (Title):

_____

What's it about?

_____

_____

_____

_____

_____

Chapter 2 (Title):

_____

What's it about?

_____

_____

_____

_____

_____

Chapter 3 (Title):

_____

What's it about?

_____

_____

_____

_____

_____

Chapter 4 (Title):

_____

What's it about?

_____

_____

_____

_____

_____

Chapter 5 (Title):

_____

What's it about?

_____

_____

_____

_____

_____

Chapter 6 (Title):

_____

What's it about?

_____

_____

_____

_____

_____

Chapter 7 (Title):

_____

What's it about?

_____

_____

_____

_____

_____

Chapter 8 (Title):

_____

What's it about?

_____

_____

_____

_____

_____

Chapter 9 (Title):

_____

What's it about?

_____

_____

_____

_____

_____

Chapter 10 (Title):

_____

What's it about?

_____

_____

_____

_____

_____

About the Author

Jevon Bolden is an editor, writer, literary agent, and CEO of Embolden Media Group, a boutique publishing consulting firm. She is best known for her work with Christian best-selling authors such as John Eckhardt, Michelle McClain-Walters, William McDowell, Don Colbert, and Cherie Calbom, a.k.a. "the Juice Lady."

She has served as senior editor for both Christian and mainstream publishers, acquiring and developing content on topics ranging from natural health and wellness to spiritual and personal growth, Christian living, and children's nonfiction. The books she has written as other people have appeared on ECPA and CBA best-seller lists and have sold hundreds of thousands of copies around the world.

Other Books by Jevon

Pray Hear Write: 21 Days to Prayer and Fasting for Breakthrough in Your Writing

Break Through Writer's Block: New Tips, Insights, and Practices to Get You Writing Again

Get Published: Seven Secrets to Getting Your Manuscript Accepted